A Practical Guide to Performance

Noodle Juice Ltd
www.noodle-juice.com
Stonesfield House, Stanwell Lane, Great Bourton, Oxfordshire, OX17 1QS
First published in Great Britain 2023
Copyright © Noodle Juice Ltd 2023
Text by Sarah Walden 2022
Illustrations by Hannah Li 2022
All rights reserved
Printed in China
A CIP catalogue record of this book is available from the British Library
ISBN: 978-1-915613-04-2
10 9 8 7 6 5 4 3 2 1

This book is made from FSC®-certified paper. By choosing this book, you help to take care of the world's forests. Learn more: www.fsc.org.

**All the world's a stage,
And all the men and women merely players;
They have their exits and their entrances,
And one man in his time plays many parts,
His acts being seven ages.**

William Shakespeare, *As You Like It*

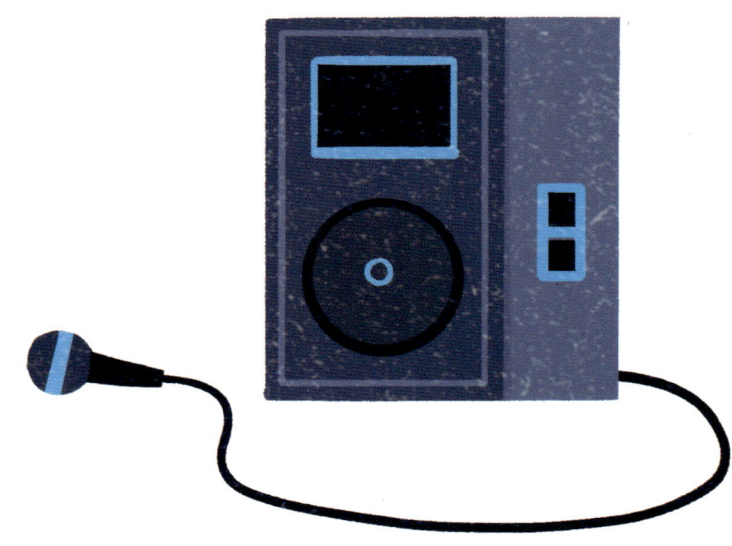

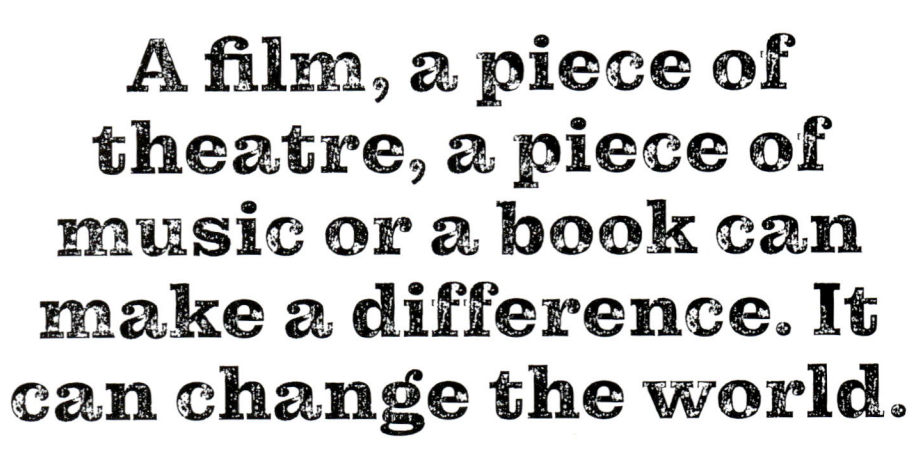

A film, a piece of theatre, a piece of music or a book can make a difference. It can change the world.

Alan Rickman, actor

Contents

6   What is performance?

8   Curtains in 3… 2… 1
10 The play's the thing
13 He's behind you!
14 A song and dance routine
18 Open mic night
20 Different stage types
24 Famous theatres

26 Cameras rollin'…
28 20th century cinema magic
30 Film genres
32 Films from around the world
34 TV and streaming
36 TV genres

38 It's not all greasepaint and applause!

40 Producer
42 Writer
44 Director
46 Set design and location
48 Costume
50 Director of photography
51 Lighting designer
52 Props
54 Actors
58 Sound and music
60 Special effects
62 Rehearsals
64 Awards ceremonies

66 How to stage your own play
70 How to make your own film
74 How to get started

76 Further reading
78 Index

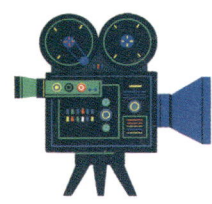

What is performance?

A performance is when someone puts on a show, a play or a spectacle to entertain an audience. It could be in a theatre, community hall or even a field.

Another type of performance is one that has been recorded or filmed, and then is shown to many people in cinemas or their own home.

The performers on stage or screen tell a story. They act out the feelings of the characters they are portraying.

Sometimes these can be happy, sometimes sad.

In ballet, the story is told only through dance.

In opera, the story is told only through song.

In musical theatre, both song and dance are combined with words to produce an amazing performance.

Films can sometimes be high-budget action adventures with famous actors, or set in the past with authentic costumes and sets.

A gritty detective series or a cookery programme are just two examples of the many types of TV shows.

There are lots of different kinds of performance and different countries have their own film and TV traditions. The entertainment industry is a fascinating world that requires a huge number of people in many different roles to make content that we can watch on our phones, computers and cinema screens or in theatres, halls and arenas.

Turn the page to discover more!

Curtains in 3...2...1

Live performance is when you act, sing or dance in front of a real or 'live' audience. There is no room for mistakes and you can't stop the performance and start again.

The show must go on.

Each member of the cast and crew have to work together to make sure the audience experiences the director's vision.

If the audience like what they see, they will applaud loudly. Sometimes they will even give a 'standing ovation', where they climb to their feet and whoop and holler to show their appreciation for what they have just enjoyed.

The play's the thing

A play is peformed on stage with actors taking different parts.

Plays are written in acts – or sections – with intervals in between. Each act is split into scenes. The most famous playwright in the world is William Shakespeare. He wrote plays with up to four acts.

Shakespeare's most famous plays

Macbeth (T)

King Lear (T)

The Tempest (C)

Romeo and Juliet (T)

Othello (T)

Hamlet (T)

A Midsummer Night's Dream (C)

As You Like It (C)

Henry V (H)

Richard III (H)

Coriolanus (T)

Troilus and Cressida (T)

The Taming of the Shrew (H)

Key

(T) Tragedies are plays where serious ideas, such as jealousy or ambition, are explored and normally nearly everyone dies.

(C) Comedies examine the lighter side of life and in theory should make you laugh.

(H) Histories portray historical events although they might not bear too much resemblence to actual fact.

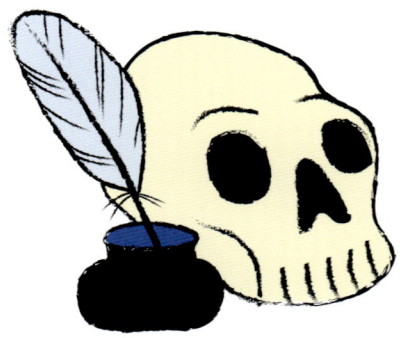

Dialogue

A play is written purely in dialogue. Each character's speech helps to tell the story. Sometimes one character speaks on stage on their own. This speech is called a monologue.

O Romeo, Romeo, wherefore art thou Romeo?

Cast List
Romeo – John
Juliet – Emma
Nurse, second soldier from the left, front half of the donkey – Hannah

The cast or dramatis personae

A cast of actors play different roles. Sometimes one actor plays more than one part.

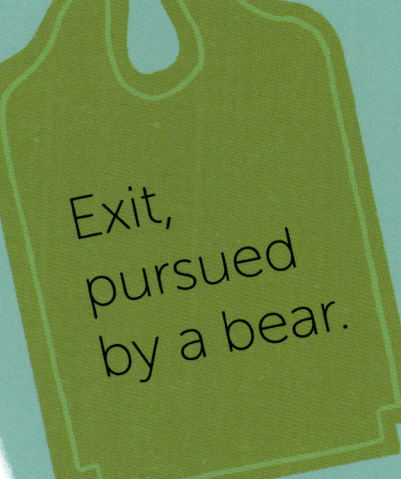

Exit, pursued by a bear.

Stage directions

The writer includes 'stage directions' in the play so that the actors know where they should be on stage, or how they should behave.

The set

The set is used to represent where the play's events are happening. Some plays have huge, movable sets that change with each scene. Other plays might just use a simple chair and table throughout the whole performance.

Theatre superstitions

Theatre people work very closely together in order to put on a performance every night. Like any community, they have their traditions, although some can seem quite eccentric.

People who work in theatre don't say 'Good luck!' to each other. They say 'break a leg'. One possible reason for this is that the curtains which separate back and front stage used to be called 'legs' and so to 'break a leg' meant you were crossing on to the stage.

It's considered bad luck to refer to Shakespeare's *Macbeth* in a theatre. Actors call it 'The Scottish Play' instead.

A bad dress rehearsal should mean a fantastic first-night performance. There's no real truth in this, other than the shock of a bad performance often encourages everyone to try their best on the opening night.

Don't ever whistle backstage. This one has its origin in fact. Stage hands used whistles as signals for moving lighting rigs or scenery. If an actor whistled backstage, they could risk setting off a cue at the wrong time.

He's behind you!

The history of pantomime or mime dates back to ancient Greek and Roman times when actors often portrayed scenes from daily life, but in an exaggerated and humorous way.

Mime now signifies how actors use their bodies to convey a message rather than speech.

It is used regularly in Chinese and Japanese theatre to convey symbolism and drama. Hindu dance-dramas also contain mime elements.

The current English pantomime tradition developed in the Victorian era when fairy tales were used as the basis for a family-friendly entertainment. Pantomimes normally run over the festive period and allow for lots of audience participation.

A song and dance routine

Musical theatre is another form of performance which seamlessly blends song and dance with a story to entertain the audience. Often musicals have fantastic sets and costumes. Many successful musicals make their way on to screens as well, so you may have seen some of these shows on TV.

A musical timeline

**Funny Face
1927**

Written by George and Ira Gershwin, this was later turned into a film starring Fred Astaire and Audrey Hepburn.

**Showboat
1927**

With music by Kern and lyrics by Oscar Hammerstein, this musical follows the lives of the performers and workers on a Mississippi River showboat.

**Oklahoma!
1943**

Written by the great pairing of Rodgers and Hammerstein, this tells the tale of farm girl Laurey Williams's courtship by two rivals, Curley and Judd. Its first run lasted for over 2,000 shows.

South Pacific
1949

Also by Rodgers and Hammerstein, this musical contains the famous songs 'I'm Gonna Wash That Man Right Outa My Hair' and 'Some Enchanted Evening'.

My Fair Lady
1957

Written by Alan Jay Lerner and Frederick Loewe, this musical tells the tale of Professor Henry Higgins who bets his friend he can transform a Cockney working-class girl into a member of high society.

West Side Story
1957

Leonard Bernstein and Stephen Sondheim collaborated to create this retelling of Shakespeare's *Romeo and Juliet* set in New York City. This was the first ever musical tragedy.

Hair
1967

One of the first rock musicals, this included loud music and flashing lights to reflect the era in which it was set.

Jesus Christ Superstar
1971

Sometimes biblical stories were set to rock music. Andrew Lloyd Webber and Tim Rice worked together to create this spectacular show.

Evita
1978

Inspired by the real-life Eva Peron, the muscial tells the story of a poor teenage girl who escapes poverty by becoming an actress and then wife of the powerful Argentinian president, Juan Peron.

Sweeny Todd
1979

Stephen Sondheim took inspiration from true crime to create this dark and critically acclaimed musical.

Cats
1981

Based on T.S. Eliots' poetry collection, *Old Possum's Book of Practical Cats*, Andrew Lloyd Webber's music ensured that the musical's first London run lasted for almost 9,000 performances.

Starlight Express
1984

A first in musical theatre, all the cast performed on roller skates. The theatre had to be rebuilt in order to accommodate skate tracks through the audience.

Les Misérables
1985

Adapted by producer Cameron Mackintosh, from the French original, which in turn is based on a classic French novel, the English stage version is the longest-running musical in London's West End.

The Lion King
1997

Written by Elton John and Tim Rice for the Disney film of the same name, this musical is well-known for its animal puppetry.

Wicked
2003

Still running today, *Wicked* tells the backstory of the Wicked Witch of the West from *The Wizard of Oz*. 'Defying Gravity' is one of the most famous musical songs today.

The Book of Mormon
2011

This musical comedy is one of the most successful musicals of all time, with huge box office sales of over $500 million.

Hamilton
2015

Written by Lin Manuel Miranda, this spectacular musical is one of the first to use rap in its musical arrangements. It tells the story of Alexander Hamilton, one of the Founding Fathers of the United States.

Six
2017

A modern retelling of the lives of the six wives of Henry VIII, this musical uses a pop concert to audition the wives for the position of the group's lead singer.

Open mic night

You don't need to have a big cast or large production to take to the stage. There are plenty of opportunities for individuals to perform. You could be a stand-up comedian, or create a one-person show. You can read poetry or perform a monologue.

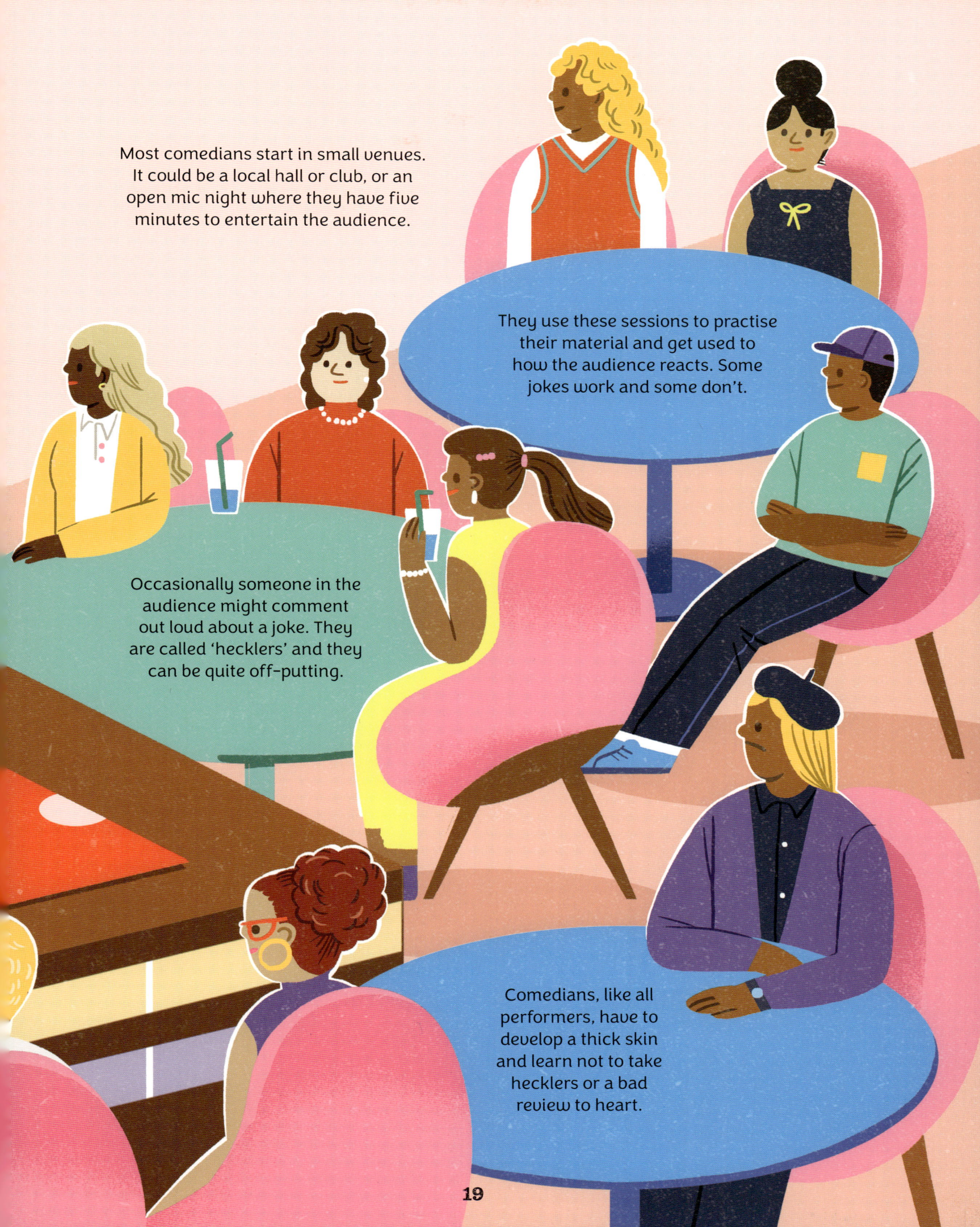

Different stage types

Proscenium stages

Most traditional theatres have a proscenium stage. Recognisable by its architectural frame, known as the proscenium arch, the stage is deep from front to back and sometimes is even raked. This means the stage is gently sloped towards the back of the stage, rising away from the audience. Sometimes the front of the stage comes forward past the proscenium into the auditorium. This is known as an apron or forestage. These theatres often have an orchestra pit for live music and a fly tower for the movement of scenery and lighting.

Thrust stages

As the name suggests, this type comes out or 'thrusts' into the auditorium with the audience sitting around the stage on three sides. The thrust stage can be square, semicircular or even half a polygon with any number of sides. These stages are used to connect the actors with the audience more closely.

Theatres in the round

The famous Globe Theatre in London is an example of this stage type and has a central performance area enclosed by the audience on most sides. Actors enter through aisles or vomitories between the seating. This staging relies almost entirely on the actors' performance as any scenery can't obstruct the audience's view.

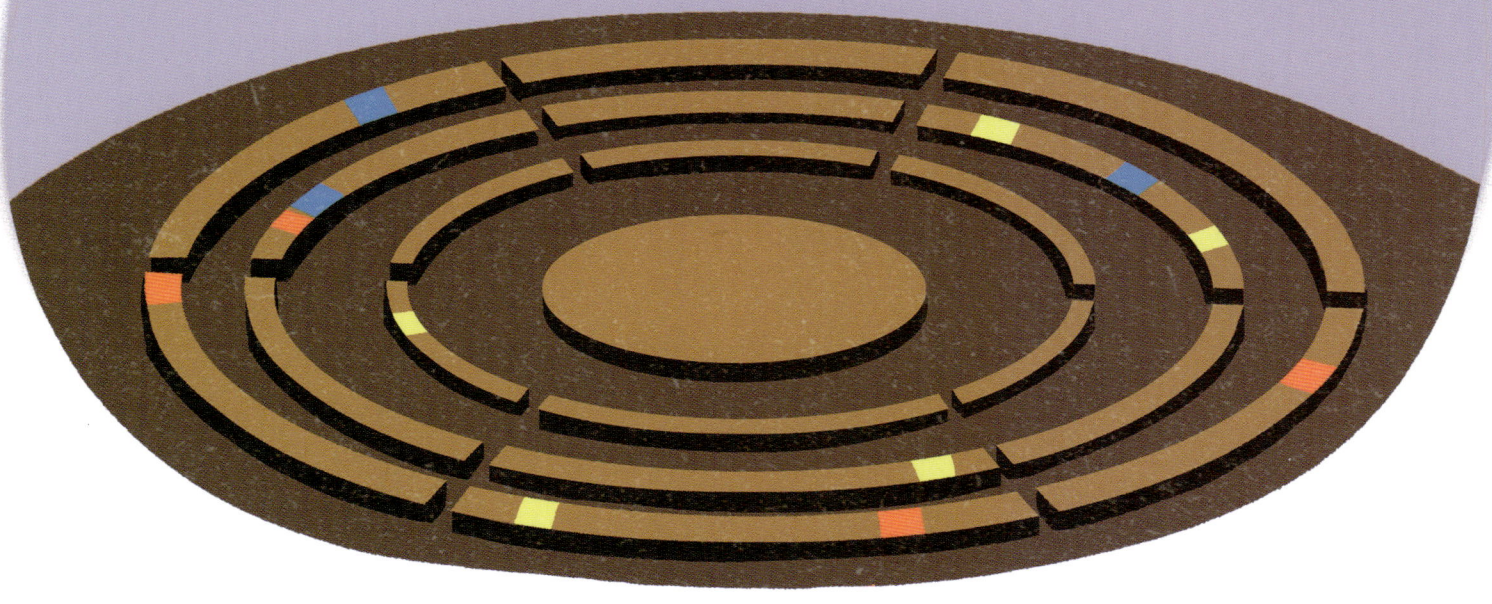

Arena theatres

Arena theatres are very big spaces that can seat large audiences. They normally have a central stage area with the audience on all sides. The stage area is usually rectangular, more like a sports arena, with tiered seating. Sometimes the stage can be circular, like the Colosseum in Rome.

Open-air theatres

These are outdoor theatres that do not have a roof, and so are dependent on the weather! Some stately homes or museums use their grounds to hold events like these. The director will try to use the changing natural light to give an atmospheric impact, especially sunset.

Studio or black box theatres

These are smaller, flexible performance spaces which are really just a single room painted black. The first row of the audience shares the floor of the stage. Normally there isn't a lot of scenery involved, and the seating can be moved around too. New or experimental theatre often starts out in a studio environment to trial an audience's reaction.

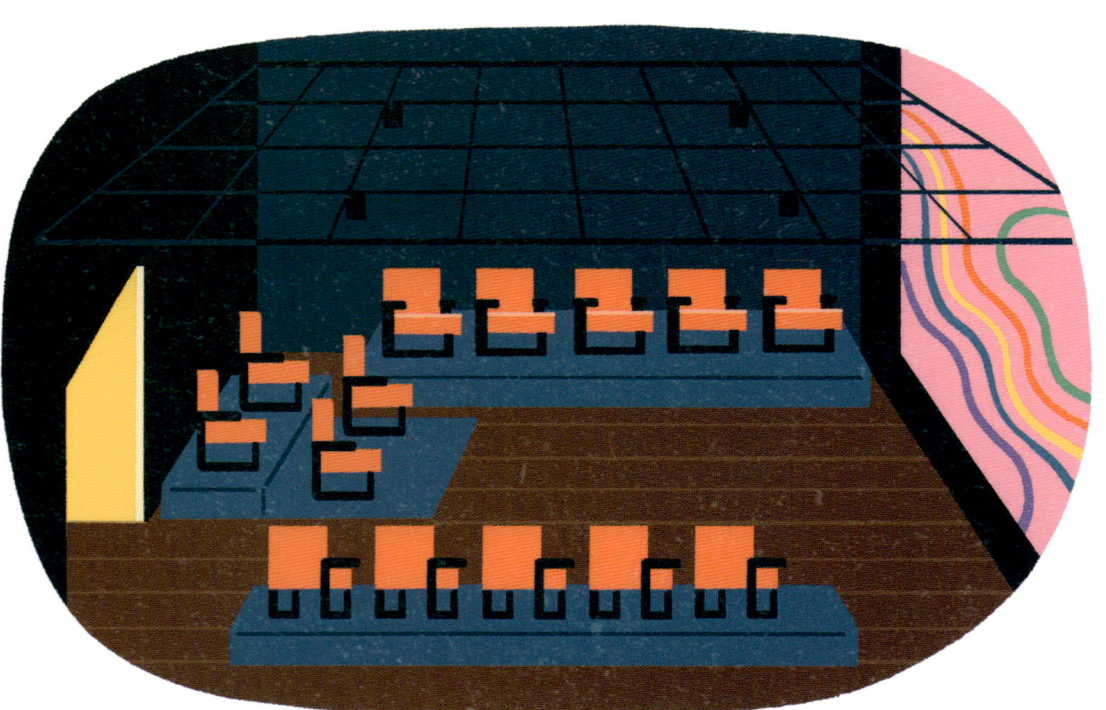

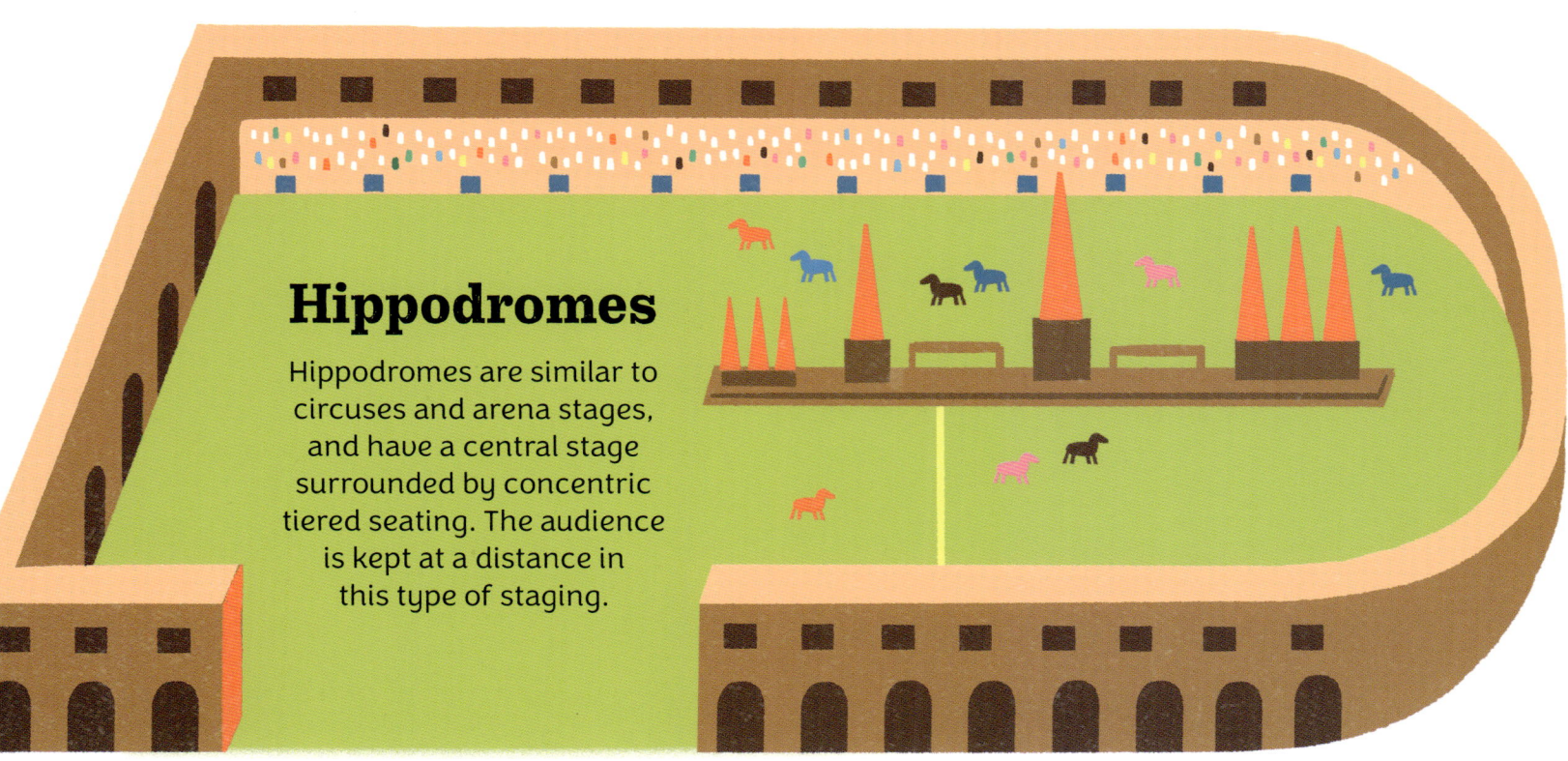

Hippodromes

Hippodromes are similar to circuses and arena stages, and have a central stage surrounded by concentric tiered seating. The audience is kept at a distance in this type of staging.

Platform theatres

This type is often found in a village or school hall where the space has multiple uses. It consists of a raised rectangular platform at one end of a room. The audience sit in rows facing the stage. Where the stage is open and without curtains, they are sometimes known as end stages or open stages.

Promenade theatre

This involves the audience moving from place to place following the actors and performance. Imagine a ghost walk through a town at night, with actors playing their roles at different points.

Famous theatres

There are theatres in most towns and cities across the globe. Most capital cities have a theatre district such as London's West End or New York's Broadway.

The very first theatre thought to have existed for the purpose of performance is the theatre of Dionysis in Athens, Greece. It was built out of stone, next to the Acropolis, in 330 BCE.

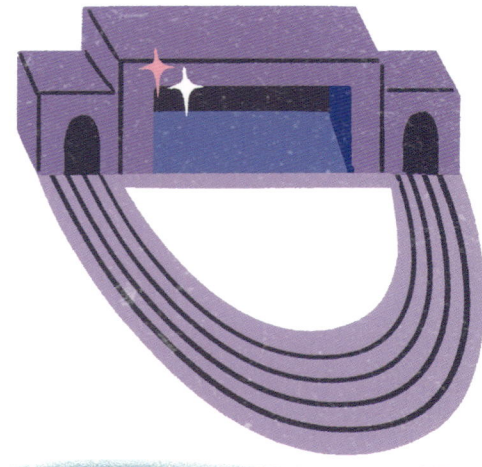

Teatro Olimpico in Vicenza, Italy, was the first permanent indoor theatre to be built. Designed by famous architect Andrea Palladio, it was completed in 1585.

London's West End contains 38 different theatres. The oldest one still in use, the Theatre Royal, Drury Lane, opened in 1663.

Teatro alla Scala in Milan, Italy is a world-famous opera house. It has hosted some of the most magnificent performers throughout history.

The Globe Theatre, London, was where Shakespeare's plays were performed during his lifetime. The 16th century building has been completely restored and now allows audiences to experience 17th century theatre.

The Comédie-Française in Paris, France, often staged plays by renowned French writers Racine, Voltaire and Molière.

The Burgtheater in Vienna, Austria, opened its doors to the public in 1888 and is the most important German-speaking theatre in the world.

The Opera House in Sydney, Australia, is one of the most modern theatres in the world. Its iconic architecture makes it instantly recognisable.

In the USA, New York's Broadway is a boulevard of many theatres. It is famous for being one of the only streets in New York that runs on a diagonal. It was also one of the first streets to have electric street lamps.

Cameras rollin'...

Another way to perform is to do so in front of a camera.

There is no audience, other than the rest of the cast and crew. The actors are filmed by up to four or five cameras at a time to make sure that the director captures everything they want to see on screen.

Sometimes, the crew film the same scene over and over again to get it right.

It can take days to make only a few short minutes of complete footage.

And ... cut! That's a wrap!

After filming, the film or TV programme will then be put together in the editing suite. This is where the director selects the best possible combination of shots to achieve their vision.

20th century cinema magic

The first true moving picture was filmed in 1877 by British-American photographer Eadweard Muybridge, who was determined to prove that a horse had all four feet off the ground when it was galloping.

Then in 1889, George Eastman, an industrialist, started manufacturing celluloid film for photography. Put those two elements together with Thomas Edison's desire to have a moving-picture element to accompany his musical phonograph, and the motion picture camera was born.

The Lumiere brothers invented the first proper projector in 1895 and their invention travelled the world, creating the idea of cinema wherever it went.

Georges Méliès is believed to be responsible for first using storytelling in cinema. Before his work, the films shown by projectionists across the world were simple scenes or one-trick shots which used stop-motion photography to miraculously remove an object from sight. Méliès made over 500 films before his death in 1912.

The first film companies appeared during the 1910s with giants such as Pathé and Gaumont Pictures dominating European film production.

Between 1910 and 1927, many hundreds of silent films were made. In the US, while producers experimented with shooting in various locations, a small town known as Hollywood started to attract attention. This was mainly due to the average 320 days a year of temperate sunshine, a wide range of geography to film in and plenty of land to build on.

D.W. Griffiths is heralded as the man who invented modern film production. He started to experiment with different camera shots and angles, as well as the editing process, to increase the impact on the audience.

During the 1920s, the motion picture industry grew hugely, creating stars such as Charlie Chaplin, Buster Keaton, Mary Pickford and Douglas Fairbanks.

Between 1927 and 1929, cinema moved into sound. Talkies, as the films became known, were incredibly popular even if the early versions were limited by microphone range and noises on set.

Walt Disney released the first animated film in 1929, using sound that synchronised perfectly with the action on screen.

Films using colour had entertained audiences from the early 1910s, but it wasn't until 1932 that Technicolour invented a primary colour process that looked realistic.

For the next 25 years, every colour film was made using Technicolour processes. Films such as *Snow White and the Seven Dwarves* (1937), *The Adventures of Robin Hood* (1938) and *The Wizard of Oz* (1939) were all made possible by Technicolour.

Famous Hollywood film studios

During the 1930s and 1940s, American film production was dominated by big film studios which not only controlled the production of films, but also where they were sold. Many of these companies still exist today.

Columbia Pictures

Metro Goldwyn Meyer (MGM)

Paramount

RKO Radio

Twentieth Century Fox

Universal Pictures

United Artists

Warner Brothers

This period was also one of censorship. During the American Depression, the Legion of Decency put pressure on film studios to adhere to a strict moral code, restricting the creativity of the industry. European and British film-making also grew during this period, creating content to satisfy their audiences at home.

After World War II, film studios started to face some challenges. In the US, there were concerns over Communist influence in the industry. The increase in television ownership also had an impact on cinema audience numbers.

Filmmakers fought back by introducing wide-screen technology that meant they could shoot on an impressive scale. The renowned director Alfred Hitchcock created his best work using this system.

Alfred Hitchcock films

Rear Window, 1954

The Man Who Knew Too Much, 1956

Vertigo, 1958

North by Northwest, 1959

Psycho, 1960

The Birds, 1963

European filmmakers made many films after World War II with directors such as Fellini and Truffaut becoming very successful. In Britain, many classic books were turned into films, such as Dickens' *Great Expectations* and Shakespeare's *Henry V*.

During the 1960s and 1970s, Britain became the film production capital of the Western world. Stanley Kubrick's *2001: A Space Odyssey* and *A Clockwork Orange* were both filmed in the UK.

After a brief decline during the 1980s, and the introduction of Film Four, the British film industry rose to even more heady heights, with international hits such as *A Room With a View* and *Four Weddings and a Funeral*.

In the US, blockbuster movies such as *Jaws, Star Wars* and *The Godfather* stimulated huge investment in cinema which continues to this day. Disney and Marvel franchises create regular box office hits.

Film genres

Starring Beverly Banana

Action
Beverly Banana is involved in a bank heist and a car chase.

Comedy
Beverly Banana slips on her own banana skin and lands face down in a cream pie.

Drama
Beverly Banana has to face up to the fact that her sister Greta Grape probably has a different father.

Fantasy
Beverly Banana enters the fruit bowl and emerges into a world made of icecream.

Horror
Beverly Banana is chased by her mouldy great-uncle Barry who has risen from the food waste bin.

Mystery
Bevely Banana has to work out who is responsible for eating all the pancakes.

Romance
Beverly Banana meets Barry Banana across a crowded fruit bowl.

Sci-Fi
Beverly Banana travels through space to Blue Banana world.

Thriller
Beverly Banana is sure that the banana next door is spying on her.

Western
Beverly Banana searches for gold with her trusty sidekick Plum.

Films from around the world

Bollywood

The centre of Hindi language film-making in India began in the 1930s. There are several different film types including the historical epic, the mythological movie and the musical. Often the stars of the films were more important than the plot and became legendary in the eyes of their fans. Today, Bollywood produces over a thousand films a year with spectacular song and dance routines and amazing costumes.

China

China, including Hong Kong, has produced the highest grossing films outside of the US. A particularly popular genre is the Hong Kong action movie featuring fantastic martial arts fight scenes.

Animé

These animated films originated in Japan in the 1950s. Inspired by manga literature, modern animé has now found an international audience, both children and adult. Characters such as Pokémon and series such as *My Hero Acadamia* have been globally successful.

TV and streaming

The first television transmission was in 1925. John Logie Baird, a British engineer, managed to transmit the image of a human face. By 1929, he had persuaded the BBC to allow him to broadcast three 30-minute shows a week.

By the 1950s, there were over 12 million black and white television sets in existence, and television companies needed to create programmes to appear on them. The first colour television set was produced in 1954, but it was much more expensive to purchase than black and white, so it didn't become commonplace until the 1960s.

The next real innovation during the 1990s was digital television – this meant not only better quality images on the screen, but many more channels on which to show programmes. That, in combination with fast internet connections, led to the ability to stream content on 'smart TVs'.

Creating content for TV was an expensive process so the first TV shows needed to be cheap to produce, with inexpensive sets. Genres that were created in response to this issue are still popular today.

Entertainment shows including comedians and musicians and their host

Sit-coms (short for situational comedy)

Westerns

Game shows

The power of TV

The ability to communicate with a large audience 24 hours a day means that television plays an important part in a country's culture.

News programmes inform their audience of daily events. Millions of people all over the world watch sports events like the Olympics or football tournaments.

Documentaries, such as *The Blue Planet*, explore serious issues like climate change.

Streaming platforms

These days, you don't need a TV to watch a TV programme. Visual content can be viewed on a mobile phone or laptop. There are many streaming platforms available and there is plenty of content to appeal to everyone.

TV genres

Some TV genres were developed as a way to make 'cheap' programming. Other genres were created as technology improved or because governments understood the power of being able to talk directly to their country's population in their own living room every day. Now there is a wide range of TV programming available. Here are some of the most popular genres.

News shows

This can include local or regional news programmes as well as national broadcasts.

Children's TV

This started as educational programming but has now developed into specific channels where parents can be happy the content their children are watching is age-appropriate.

Sports broadcasts

Normally, these events are shown live and achieve some of the highest viewing figures.

Cartoons

Animated programmes are not just for children. Some of the most successful cartoons, such as *The Simpsons*, appeal to the whole family.

Docudramas

Based on a true story, these shows dramatise what happened to entertain the audience.

Reality TV

Normally featuring members of the public in either a competition or demonstrating expertise in something such as cookery or home DIY, this format has become very popular in the 21st century.

Police procedurals

Incredibly popular, this genre has many different approaches, but always focuses on solving a crime through investigation.

Soap operas

The name comes from the companies that used to advertise their washing powder during these programmes to housewives in the 1950s. The slightly over-the-top plotlines and romantic dramas were often shown during the day.

Game shows

These shows usually include members of the public competing to answer general knowledge questions or complete activities for a prize.

Panel shows

A combination of a game show and a talk show, panel shows often include comedians or celebrities discussing current affairs.

Talk shows

High-profile talk show hosts interview guests and discuss topics of the moment.

Zoom IN

It's not all greasepaint and applause!

There are many different careers in theatre, TV and film! It takes more than just an actor to put a show together. How many of these roles do you recognise?

- Producer
- Director  
- Writer 
- Set designer 
- Director of photography 
- Location manager

Lighting designer

Costume designer

Prop designer

Stage manager

Floor manager

Actors

Composer

Sound engineer

Special effects artist

Visual effects artist

Find out about all these different careers on the following pages! What would you like to do?

39

Zoom IN

Producer

The producer is the starting point of the production. They often spot the creative opportunity and then work with writers to create the script. They also raise financial investment from backers, hire the director and have input into the casting and design of the show.

The producer makes the final decision on everything. They are also legally responsible for the health and safety of everyone involved in the production.

Producers have to spot and solve potential problems. They also need to make sure they have created a good working environment and they constantly talk to their team to check that everything is on track and on schedule.

What skills do you need to be a producer?

You must understand how to make a film or stage a play.

You should be good at storytelling.

You need to understand the numbers.

You should be good at communication.

You should be able to lead a team.

You absolutely have to be organised.

Zoom IN: Writer

The playwright or scriptwriter is where the story starts, whether it is for stage or screen. They are responsible for creating the story and the characters. They decide where and when the story is set. They work closely with the producer and director to make sure their story can be turned into a visual performance.

Writers can create a script from an original idea or by adapting an existing idea (from a book or real-life experience).

Sometimes writers are asked to join an existing project or series. TV shows will often have several writers working together.

Things to remember when writing a screenplay

1. Create a great world to set your story. Think about where and when you want your characters to live and breathe.

2. Choose a theme that matters to you. You need to convince your audience.

3. Work out what your hook is – why an audience will want to watch your production.

4. Pick a genre and stick to it. Don't mix them up. If you want to write a comedy, you probably don't need scary zombies.

5. Make sure there is an unresolvable problem that your hero keeps trying to fix, but never quite achieves. It keeps your audience on the edge of their seat.

6. It is a good idea to storyboard out the key scenes so you know exactly what shots you require from the film crew.

What skills do you need to be a writer?

You need to understand how to write well for stage or screen.

You must be creative. Originality is key.

You should be interested in theatre, film and TV.

You must be self-motivated as you often have to find your own work opportunities.

You must be able to handle constructive criticism and editorial feedback.

Zoom IN

Director

The director takes the script and turns the story into a visual production. In theatre, the director devises the staging and works with actors to ensure they understand their characters and deliver their lines correctly.

The director also works with the set and costume designers, as well as lighting and sound, to make sure that the surroundings work with the actors' performance. In film and TV, they have a much bigger backdrop to work with, and multiple camera angles to consider.

A director works with casting directors to choose the actor for each part. They then 'block' each scene so the director knows where each actor should be at every minute, how they move around and how they will perform their lines.

After a stage performance, a director will give 'notes' to the cast. They might decide to change the way a line is delivered or position an actor in a different place.

For a film or TV director, once they have finished filming on set, they still need to edit the film to create the final 'cut', which must be approved by the producer. This is where the soundtrack and any special effects are added to the film to complete the director's vision.

What skills do you need to be a director?

You need to be able to lead a team and share your vision for the production.

You have to have a great imagination so you can see exactly what you're trying to create.

You should be interested in theatre, film and TV.

You must be able to stay calm under pressure and react well if problems occur.

You should understand the production process and how it impacts on what you do.

Zoom IN

Set design and location

A set designer creates the look of a set for a theatre production. These can be hugely elaborate moving sets or a simple backdrop and furniture.

They need to be practical too, as they have to take into account the director's vision and make it become a reality.

A location manager is responsible for finding a physical place that matches the director's vision for the look and feel of the film. They might be looking for a jungle, an underground car park or a stately home.

They need to make sure that whatever they find is easy to get to, safe and won't cost too much to hire.

What skills do you need to be a set designer?

You need to be creative and understand how to transform a director's vision into reality.

Drawing skills are helpful.

You should be good at solving problems, planning and time-management.

You must be a team player.

What skills do you need to be a location manager?

You need to have an eye for landscape and architecture and be able to visualise how a location would work as a film set.

You must be good with a camera to take pictures of the locations you discover.

You should be a good negotiator and be aware of health and safety legislation.

You must be organised and a good communicator.

Zoom IN

Costume

Costumes are an important part of building a character for the audience. They also help the actors to connect with their roles.

The costume designer works with the director to understand their vision for the performance. They are responsible for the design, creation and hiring of all the costumes used on set or on stage.

Period costume needs to be carefully researched. If a detail isn't correct, it can spoil the whole look of the film, TV show or play.

For professional theatre productions, costumes are washed after every performance. This means that they must be hard-wearing. Actors usually have multiple sets of their costume.

There are as many different types of costume as there are types of film. Designers need to source all sorts of different materials and embellishments to create fantastic outfits. Think of a knight in armour, or a beautiful ball gown. What about a superhero costume or an alien? The costume designer has to create them all.

What skills do you need to be a costume designer?

You need to have an eye for style and be able to interpret the director's vision.

You must understand clothing design throughout history and be able to research details.

You need to understand how colours work together and how they can tell a story.

You should know how clothes are put together and how to make them.

You must be organised and a good communicator.

Zoom IN

Director of photography

In film and TV, the director of photography is responsible for filming the action on set.

They work closely with the director and lighting designer to work out how to create the desired look and feel of the film. A desert sky will need a different approach to an underground car park.

It's not just about lighting though, it's also about how each shot is framed – a close-up of an actor's face, or a long shot that shows perspective can all change the mood of the film.

What skills do you need to be a director of photography?

You need to understand photography, have an eye for composition and be able to tell a story with an image.

You should be good with cameras, lenses, monitors and lights.

You must understand how the editing process works and be able to make decisions quickly.

It's important to be a good communicator and be very organised.

Zoom IN

Lighting designer

The lighting on a stage or set is important. The lighting designer works closely with the director of photography in films and TV, and with the director in theatre.

The designer uses lighting effects to persuade the audience that it's night-time, or that something dangerous might be coming. Lighting helps to change the mood on stage, or signal a change in location.

What skills do you need to be a lighting designer?

You need to have excellent colour vision and be able to interpret what the director wants.

You need to understand the technical requirements of the lighting desk.

You need to work well under pressure and be able to make quick decisions.

Zoom IN

Props

Prop masters are responsible for sourcing all the different elements used in productions, such as jewellery, weapons or even moving models. They work closely with the production team to make sure that the props look authentic and match the period of the show.

Props can be small, such as a wine glass, which can be bought or hired easily, or they can be large, such as an aircraft or a tank. Props of this size often need to be created on set by carpenters, artists and prop makers. The prop master is responsible for co-ordinating this process, as well as managing the props budget.

During a stage performance, the prop master is responsible for making sure that each prop is exactly where it needs to be when the actor needs it. Once the prop has been used, it is returned to the props cupboard ready for the next performance.

Imagine a performance of *Hamlet* without Yorick's skull!

Alas, poor Yorick. I knew him well.

The prop master is key to making sure there is continuity throughout a film or play. Was the actor carrying an umbrella in the last scene? Where is it now?

What skills do you need to be a prop master?

You should be able to work through a script and identify the props required.

You need to be practical and be able to work with lots of different materials.

You should have good historical knowledge to ensure there are no digital watches in a 17th century play!

You must be able to manage budgets, schedules, transport and storage.

Zoom IN

Floor or stage manager

A stage manager supports and manages all the teams involved in the day-to-day production of the show, from rehearsals through to the final performance. On a TV set, they are called the floor manager, but have a similar role.

A floor manager is responsible for helping to plan and prepare the TV programme. They supervise the setting up of any equipment such as microphones or props. They will then run sound and lighting checks to make sure everything is working properly.

Once the show is live, the floor manager gives cues and time counts to the people on set. If there is a studio audience, the floor manager is responsible for telling them what to do.

The floor manager is also responsible for health and safety on set.

A stage manager will create the rehearsal schedules for cast and crew. They will manage set furniture and props and arrange costume and wig fittings.

They supervise the 'get in' and 'get out' of the theatre and make sure that the set, lighting and sound are correctly installed.

They manage any scene and prop changes during the show and cue the lighting and sound technicians.

The stage manager also looks after the health and safety of the whole cast and crew.

What skills do you need to be a floor or stage manager?

You must be extremely good at organisation and communication.

You need to be decisive and quick to solve problems.

You should have a good understanding of the techinical side of the production, and equipment being used.

You must be physically active and able to move quietly.

Zoom IN

Actors

An actor's role is more complicated than you might think. Often considered the headline role in any production, most actors work incredibly hard for little reward. Of course, there are very famous actors who are paid large fees to appear in films, TV series or on stage. Most actors, however, need to take a second job to support themselves in between roles.

Once cast in a role, a stage actor has to do the following:

- Research the play or character
- Learn lines, songs or dances
- Make sure they attend all rehearsals, including technical and dress rehearsals
- Work with the costume department
- Respond to the director's requests, and learn what props they are using
- Perform seven performances a week (five evening shows and two matinées)

A TV or film actor only has to perform until the director is happy with the take!

Auditions

To get a part in a film, show or play, most actors have to attend auditions with a casting director.

An audition is when you demonstrate how well you can perform. Sometimes you might read from a script, or you can perform something you have prepared earlier.

Actors often attend dozens of auditions before getting their first break.

More famous actors are sometimes invited to audition or be part of the production. These actors will usually have agents who work on their behalf.

NEXT!

What skills do you need to be an actor?

You should be confident in front of an audience and comfortable performing.

You must be able to take direction.

You must be able to interpret your lines and deliver them well.

You should work well as a team, but also on your own.

You need to be reliable and have good time-keeping skills.

Zoom IN

Sound and music

Sound is very important to performance. The sound designer is responsible for all the sound effects, either recorded or live, for a stage performance. In TV and film, sound is often added in post-production and this increases the impact of what is on screen.

Sound effects can be simple, such as a door creaking open or a phone ringing. But it is still important to make sure these are cued properly and happen at exactly the right time in the performance.

Other sound effects can be complicated and difficult to create. A thunderstorm, for example, or the sound of a battle. These will be created and recorded before the performance.

There are digital libraries of sound effects that can be licensed for use. The sound designer is responsible for that budget.

Some shows don't include music, but they are very few. Even if the show isn't a musical, there will often be background music to help sustain the mood on stage or on the set.

Famous composers of film scores, such as Hans Zimmer or John Williams, have very recognisable styles.

In large stage productions, the music director conducts the orchestra every night. In smaller shows, the music is recorded and cued by the sound technician.

What skills do you need to work in sound?

You must be able to use a sound-editing programme and sound equipment.

You should be creative and able to think outside the box when creating sound effects.

You should be aware of different sound libraries and where to source different sound effects.

You need to be reliable and have good time-keeping skills.

Zoom IN

Special effects

The special effects department can be one of the most creative places to work. You need a T-Rex to storm down a highway? Or a twister to destroy a farm building? That's where the special effects designers come in.

During the 20th century, special effects had to be made by hand. Miniature model sets represented far-distant planets or downtown Manhattan. Car explosions were real cars blown up with real explosives. Stuntmen would jump off buildings and land on mattresses below. These effects were expensive to create and film – and often a director only got one take.

What skills do you need to be a special effects artist?

You need a love of illusion and performance.

You should be creative, artistic and able to stick to a brief.

You should have practical skills such as engineering, architecture, sculpture, puppetry or make-up.

Computer graphic imagery (CGI) has been used in film-making since the 1950s to add special effects in post-production. Directors took advantage of the new technology, but it was expensive to use.

By the 21st century, computer graphics had become very sophisticated and much cheaper to produce. These days, there are very few films produced without using CGI in some way. The technology allows directors opportunities to create new worlds without limitations.

Visual FX artists and animators create 2D or 3D models or animations using computer graphics. They also create other visual effects, such as explosions or rivers of lava.

Green screen

Now many scenes are shot in front of a green screen. The green screen is then digitally removed and the action can be dropped on to whatever background you like.

A green screen can also be used to capture human movements that are then applied to animated characters.

Why is it green?

Because green is the least like skin tone.

What skills do you need to be a visual effects artist?

You must be able to use digital animation and illustration programmes.

You should be creative, artistic and able to stick to a brief.

You need to be able to deliver your work on schedule.

You must collaborate well with others.

Zoom IN

Rehearsals

Creating an amazing performance takes a lot of people in many different roles all working hard together. Often the first time the cast and crew meet each other is at rehearsal.

There are six key types of rehearsal for a stage performance.

Reading

This is the first and most important rehearsal that the cast and crew attend. The director will set out their vision for the show and explain how they want the cast to perform.

Blocking

This is when the director plans how the cast move around the stage in response to the script. They focus on how the cast are grouped on stage and the visual impact of those groupings.

Working

As the name suggests, this is the part where it becomes hard work. The cast develop the show together, learning lines and movement. They also experiment with pace.

Polishing

At this point in the rehearsal schedule, the cast and technical crew should be running through the whole show with complete concentration. They all know what they're doing and can sense how good a performance it will be.

Technical

This rehearsal is mainly for the sound, lighting and props crew. The actors are involved, but it can be very stop and start while the technical teams refine their part in the show.

Dress

The dress rehearsal is when the cast is in full costume for the very first time. The show is run through from top to bottom, as if it were in front of an audience. The director will only stop a dress rehearsal if something has gone very wrong.

TV and film productions will have a shorter schedule with less working and polishing rehearsals, as they get to reshoot if the director isn't happy with the finished result.

Zoom IN

Awards ceremonies

After all that hard work, it's nice to be able to celebrate the greatest performances of the year. There are many different awards ceremonies for stage and screen, but here are some examples of the most famous.

The Oscars

The Academy Awards, known as the Oscars, are the most prestigious awards in the film industry. They celebrate both artistic and technical merit and it is hugely significant if you win one. Normally held in Los Angeles, USA, in March, they started in 1929. As the guests arrive, the press are keen to capture their outfits and thoughts before the results are announced.

The Golden Globes

Held in January each year, and seen as a precursor to the Oscars, the Golden Globe Awards also celebrate US and International television.

The Cannes Film Festival

This festival awards the *Palme d'Or* to what it judges to be the best international film.

The BAFTAs

The British Academy Film Awards started in 1949. Usually held in February, they also signal what might happen at the Oscars.

The Tony Awards

The Antoinette Perry Awards for Excellence in Broadway Theatre, or 'Tony' for short, celebrate live Broadway theatre. They are held to be the equivalent of the Oscars for New York theatre.

The Olivier Awards

The UK's equivalent of the Tony Awards are named after Laurence Olivier, a well-known British actor. The awards cover all West End productions and include not only plays, but musicals, dance and opera.

The Molière Awards

These are the national theatre awards of France, which began in 1987. There are thirteen awards given to productions, individual actors, directors, writers, set designers and costume designers.

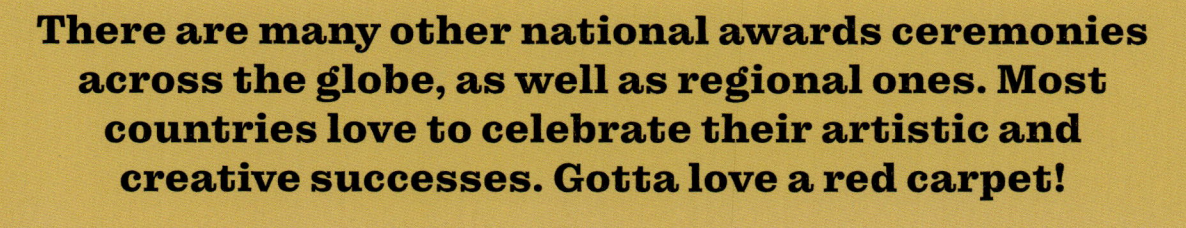

There are many other national awards ceremonies across the globe, as well as regional ones. Most countries love to celebrate their artistic and creative successes. Gotta love a red carpet!

How to stage your own play

Now you've learned all about what it takes to put on a play, it's your turn. Follow these step-by-step instructions and you'll be wowing those audiences in no time.

1. Choose your play

There are lots of plays available for you to choose from (just make sure you have permission to perform it – check with a grown-up in case you need to ask for written permission). Or write your own.

2. Choose your venue

Once you know which play you're going to perform, you need to find somewhere to perform it. If the play has a large cast, you might need a school hall or sports hall with a stage. If it's a smaller set, then a studio theatre or drama room at school could work.

3. Select your dates

Your chosen venue might dictate when you can put on your play, but you also need to plan enough time for rehearsals, set construction, costumes and props, as well as publicity to make sure your audience knows about it!

4. Hold your auditions

Find somewhere to hold your auditions – a classroom or local community centre would work well. Advertise your audition times and location. Ask your friends and family to tell everyone they know to make sure you get a good pool of actors.

5. Choose your cast

Take time before choosing your cast – you might want to do callbacks if you have two people you like for the same role. Let the successful candidates know and tell them what the rehearsal schedule looks like.

6. Appoint your production team

You will need a set designer, costume designer, lighting and sound technicians and a prop master. You will also need a stage manager to handle the team and the show on the night. In small productions, people often wear more than one hat!

7. Start rehearsing (see pages 62–63)

At the read through, make sure everyone knows each other and what role they play. It's a good idea to play some ice-breaker games if some of the cast and crew don't know each other.

8. Rehearsal etiquette

Once you're in full swing, it's important to make sure you rehearse each scene of the play thoroughly. Giving positive feedback to your cast is important, as you'll need to ask them to work hard. Sometimes bringing treats such as fruit or sweets to reward hard work works wonders.

9. Set and costumes

While the cast are rehearsing, your production team should be working on the set, lighting and costumes. You should be able to borrow most of what you need from friends and family. If you are going for an elaborate set, then you might need grown-up help to make sure it's safe. You'll need to think about stage make-up too, as strong lighting can wash out your actors' faces.

10. Lighting and sound

The venue you have chosen should have some lights that you can use. Find out what is available and work out how best to use them in each scene. Sound can be put together on a computer and then played on the night at the right time by the sound crew. Make sure you have permission to use the sound effects you need. There are many free sound effects you can download online.

11. Sell those tickets

There is no point putting on a play if there is no audience. You need to make people aware that the play is happening. Ask friends and family to put up posters around the community. Encourage them to sell tickets for a reasonable price. You may need to recover the cost of hiring the venue or costumes. Once you've covered your costs, you could donate the rest of the profits to a charity of your choice.

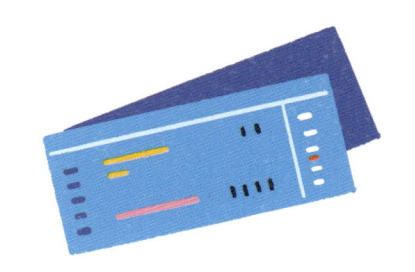

12. Technical rehearsal

It's time to run through the whole show with the sound and lighting crew to make sure they understand their cues, as well as getting the effect you want.

13. Dress rehearsal

Full cast and crew run-through of the production. As a director, you're hoping everything runs smoothly and it gives you an opportunity to make any final little tweaks. Don't change too much though, as it could be confusing for your cast at this stage.

14. Create your programme

It's usual to have a programme available at the show to credit the cast and crew, as well as thanking anyone who has helped with the production. If you've taken photographs during the dress rehearsal, it's nice to include them in the programme too.

15. Brief your front of house team

These are the people who are responsible for looking after your audience. So make sure that they know how long the first half is going to be, how long your interval is, and if there are any special requirements for the audience. Do the show need an interactive audience? The front of house team can encourage people to join in.

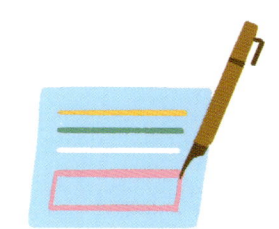

16. It's showtime!

Here you go! All your hard work, and that of your cast and crew, has been building up to this moment. Curtain's up! Break a leg!

17. The curtain call

You've had a successful show. The audience are on their feet clapping in appreciation. It's time for the curtain call. This needs organising so that the cast know who goes on first and in what order. Usually, you start with the chorus, or the people with the smaller parts in groups. They then move to either side of the stage, and the rest of the cast come on in order of importance. Finally, there is a group bow at the end before the cast leave the stage.

18. The get out

After the final show, there's still work to be done. The set needs to be broken down and removed from the venue. All the costumes and props need to be returned. The ticket sales need adding up and the proceeds shared with the right people. It's all hands to the deck.

19. The after-show party

Finally, there's a tradition which is a lot of fun! The after-show party where everyone involved in the production comes together to celebrate the success of the show. It can happen after the get out, but sometimes it's more sensible to plan the party a few days later when everyone has recovered from the run. Have fun!

How to make your own film

If you've ever dreamed of walking the red carpet at an awards ceremony, then here's the place to start. Follow these steps to create your own short film and see if you've got what it takes!

1. Choose your story

What is your hook? What story do you want to tell? Be practical in your ambitions. You are unlikely to be able to create a pirate ship or fantasy jungle in your back garden or school hall, so pick your themes and environment wisely.

2. Write your screenplay

Focus on the dialogue between characters first. Then add in the directions and location suggestions. Is there enough excitement or tension? Where is the jeopardy or emotion?

3. It's time to storyboard!

This is a really useful tool to help you visualise how the action will look on screen. You can play around with camera shots – close-up or tracking – to give you the best impact.

4. Hold your auditions

Find somewhere to hold your auditions – a classroom or local community centre would work well. Advertise your audition times and location. Depending on the scale of the production, you might want 'extras' – people who appear on screen, but who don't have any lines.

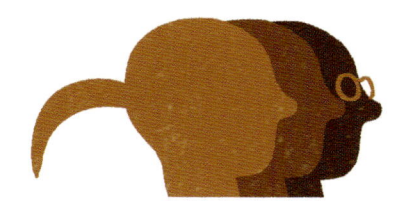

5. Choose your cast

Take time before choosing your cast – you might want to do callbacks if you have two people you like for the same role. It is worth taking test shots to see how your chosen actors look on screen. Let the successful candidates know and tell them what the filming schedule looks like.

6. Appoint your production team

You will need a locations manager, costume designer, lighting and sound technicians and a prop master. You will also need an assistant director to handle the team while filming and most importantly, someone to operate the cameras. Mobile phone cameras will work perfectly for your first film. In small productions, people often wear more than one hat, so you might be producer, director and in charge of a camera!

7. Share the script!

While film productions don't have the same rehearsal requirements as a play, it's a good idea to give the script to the actors and production team as soon as possible, so they understand what you want them to do.

8. Locations and costumes

While the cast are rehearsing, your production team should be working on finding the filming locations, lighting and costumes. For most of what you need, you should be able to borrow items from friends and family. Make sure you have permission to film in the locations you have selected if they are not public property. You must also have permission to film anyone you use, even if they are in the background.

9. Lighting and sound

Once you know your locations, your lighting and sound technicians can plan what they need. Outside filming can be tricky as there may be ambient sound, such as road noise. You might decide to get up early to film when there is less traffic around. If you want to film at night, you'll need lighting to make sure you can see your actors on camera.

10. Filming etiquette

Once you've worked out your filming schedule, it's important that everyone sticks to it and turns up when they are supposed to. Time is money in Hollywood, and it will be the same for your production too. Make sure you have reminded your cast and crew where and when they need to be on set.

11. Rehearsals

Before you shoot each scene, ask your actors to rehearse their dialogue and actions so you can make sure you have the right camera angles. You may want to give them some final notes on their performance too. You will probably repeat the same scene several times until you're happy with it. It is easy to watch it back though.

12. Film those scenes

In most film shoots, you may well end up shooting scenes out of order because it makes more sense to shoot everything in one location at the same time. It's important to remember who is wearing what at any point during the film so you don't end up with continuity errors!

13. File, file file!

Work through your shooting list methodically saving your video files with the scene number, camera and take. When you edit the recordings together, you may well use more than one so it is good to be organised with the information and know where the files are saved.

14. Into the editing suite

Now you have all your footage saved, it's time to put it together. There are some really good free editing programmes available that even include special effects and music libraries, so you can make your production look professional. They take time to learn how to use properly though, so keep trying if you don't get it right the first time.

15. Title sequence and credits

These elements top and tail a film and are important. The title sequence helps to set audience expectations and the credits allow you to celebrate everyone's hard work. It's amazing what you can do with a laptop, so have fun and be creative.

16. Your premiere!

You have a film. Well done! Now you need people to see it. Why not host a screening for friends and family of the cast and crew? That would be a lovely way to say thank you to everyone who helped you.

17. The wider audience

There are many streaming platforms where you can upload video content with your parent or guardian's approval, so if you want to share your film with a larger audience you can. Or keep this film as your first showreel, ready to demonstrate your passion for film.

How to get started...

There are lots of ways to get involved in putting on a performance.

If your school doesn't already have a drama club, why not see if you can start one?

There are organisations such as Stagecoach that will let you have a trial session to see if you want to join in on the performance side of things.

If you're more interested in the technical or back stage areas, then approach your local theatre or college to find out what workshops they offer.

You can do so much online too. There are some fabulous resources (see page 76 & 77) that will give you even more information than this book does.

Do you want to write the next best screenplay to win an Oscar?

Would you like to create an amazing set for a play?

Would you like to record the best possible soundtrack for a film?

Why not storyboard the next few years of your life?

What does a film of your life look like?

Be inspired, be creative, be organised.

But most of all, get involved and keep trying.

Further reading

There are plenty of really fabulous websites with lots more resources than we could fit into this book. Check out the following:

www.screenskills.com

www.getintotheatre.org

www.intofilm.org

www.theatrecraft.org

www.careers.broadway

www.nyfa.edu/student resources

Acknowledgements

With thanks to the following people:

Stagecoach Banbury principal Melissa Lewis, for being kind enough to read through this and check for errors. Any remaining are entirely down to the writer!

My daughter Megan, who has supported me in our musical theatre addiction.

Choreographer Steve 'Sparkle, Sparkle, Sparkle', who insisted I could transform from the Ugly Duckling into a swan all those decades ago, and who sparked my love of all things theatrical.

Newcastle University Theatre Society (NUTS) 1992–1995 who allowed me to thoroughly enjoy myself in a directorial debut and then who even more madly did it again for our production of *The Crucible* in 1994.

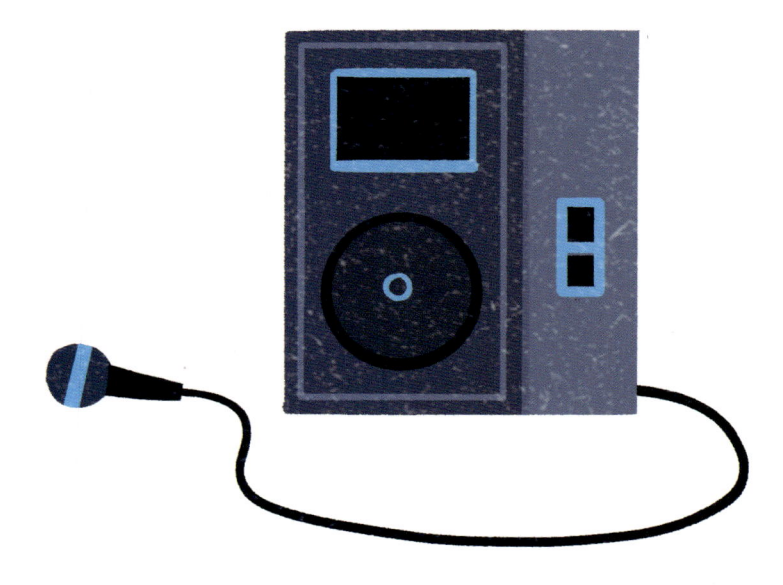

Index

Page numbers such as 14–17 show page ranges, where you will find information about the topic on all the pages between page 14 and page 17.

action films 7, 32, 33
actor (job role and skills) 56–57
after-show party 69
ancient Greek theatres 24
animé films 33
applause 8, 69
arena theatres 21
audience participation 13, 19
audience seating in theatres 20–23
auditions 57, 66, 70
awards ceremonies 64–65

BAFTAs (film awards) 65
black-box theatres 22
blocking 45, 62
Bollywood films 33
Book of Mormon, The (musical theatre) 17
British film industry 30, 31
Broadway theatres (New York) 25, 65
Burgtheater (theatre) 25

Cannes Film Festival 64
careers (job roles and skills) 40–61
cartoons (TV) 36
cast (actors) in plays 11
casting 40, 45, 57, 67, 71
Cats (musical theatre) 16
censorship 30
children's TV shows 36
Chinese film industry 33

Chinese theatre 13
cinema and film 28–33, 70–73
closing credits (film) 73
Colosseum (theatre) 21
colour in films 29–30
comedian performers 18–19
Comédie-Française (theatre) 25
comedy films 32
comedy TV shows 34
cookery TV shows 7, 37
costumer designer (job role and skills) 48–49
credits (film) 73
curtain call 69

dance 6, 13
dialogue in plays 11
Dionysis theatre 24
director (job role and skills) 44–45
director of photography (job role and skills) 50
Disney films 29, 30, 31
docudramas (TV) 36
documentaries (TV) 35
drama (film genre) 32
dress rehearsal (theatre) 63

editing films 26, 29, 45, 73
European film industry 28, 30, 31
Evita (musical theatre) 16

famous theatres 21, 24–25
fantasy films 32
film and cinema 28–33, 70–73
film editing 17, 26, 29, 45, 73
film genres 32
film (making your own film) 70–73
filming techniques 26, 29, 31, 50, 61
floor manager (job role and skills) 54, 55
front of house team (theatre) 69

Funny Face (musical theatre) 14

game shows (TV) 34, 37
genres of film 32
genres of TV 34, 36–37
Globe, The (theatre) 21, 25
Golden Globe Awards (film) 64
green screen 61

Hair (musical theatre) 15
Hamilton (musical theatre) 17
Hindu dance-dramas 13
hippodromes 23
historical dramas 7, 31, 48, 49
history of cinema and film 28–31
history of television 34
Hitchcock films 31
Hollywood film studios 29, 30
horror films 32
how to make your own film 70–73
how to stage your own play 66–69

Indian film industry 33

Japanese film industry 33
Japanese theatre 13
Jesus Christ Superstar (musical theatre) 15

La Scala (opera house) 24
Les Misérables (musical theatre) 16
lighting designer (job role and skills) 51
lighting your own film 71
lighting your own play 68
Lion King, The (musical theatre) 17
location manager (job role and skills) 46, 47
London theatres 21, 24, 25

Macbeth (theatre superstition) 12
mime 13
Molière Awards (theatre) 65
music composers (for film) 59
music directors 59
musical theatre 6, 14–17
My Fair Lady (musical theatre) 15
mystery films 32

news programmes (TV) 35, 36

Oklahoma! (musical theatre) 14
Olivier Awards (theatre) 65
open-air theatres 22
open mic nights 18–19
opera 6, 24
orchestra pits in theatres 20
Oscars (film awards) 64
outdoor theatres 21, 22, 23

Palme d'Or (film award) 64
panel shows (TV) 37
pantomime 13
period dramas 7, 31, 48, 49
platform theatres 23
plays 8–12, 66–69
plays (staging your own play) 66–69
police procedurals (TV) 37
producer (job role and skills) 40–41
programmes (theatre) 68
promenade (walking) theatres 23
prop master (job role and skills) 52–53
props 52–53, 54, 55
proscenium stages 20

reading and resources 74, 76
reality TV shows 37
rehearsals (theatre) 55, 62–63, 67
rehearsals (TV and film) 63, 72

Roman theatres 21
romance films 32
Romeo and Juliet (play) 10, 11

scene blocking 45, 62
Sci-Fi (science fiction) films 32
set designer (job role and skills) 46, 47
sets for plays 11, 46
SFX (special effects) 60–61
Shakespeare's plays 10, 11, 12
Showboat (musical theatre) 14
Six (musical theatre) 17
soap operas (TV) 37
sound designer (job role and skills) 58–59
sound effects 58, 68
South Pacific (musical theatre) 15
special effects 60–61, 73
special effects artist (job role and skills) 60
sports TV shows 36
stage directions in plays 11
stage manager (job role and skills) 54, 55
stage sets for plays 11, 46
stage types for theatres 20–23
Starlight Express (musical theatre) 16
storyboarding 43, 70
streaming TV content 34, 35
studio audiences (for TV shows) 54
studio theatres 22
superstitions about the theatre 12
Sweeny Todd (musical theatre) 16
Sydney Opera House (theatre) 25

talk shows (TV) 37
talkies (early films with sound) 29
Teatro alla Scala (opera house) 24
Teatro Olimpico (theatre) 24
technical rehearsal (theatre) 63, 68

Technicolour film processes 29–30
television genres 34, 36–37
television shows 7, 34, 35
theatre (musicals) 6, 14–17
theatre (plays) 8–12, 66–69
theatre stages and seating 20–23
theatre superstitions 12
theatres in the round 21
thrillers (films) 32
thrust stages 20
ticket selling 68, 69
title sequence (film) 73
Tony Awards (theatre) 65
TV shows 7, 34, 35

US film industry 29–30, 31

visual effects artist (job role and skills) 61

West End theatres 16, 24, 65
West Side Story (musical theatre) 15
westerns (films) 32
westerns (TV shows) 34
whistling backstage (theatre superstition) 12
writer (job role and skills) 42–43
writing tips 42–43, 70

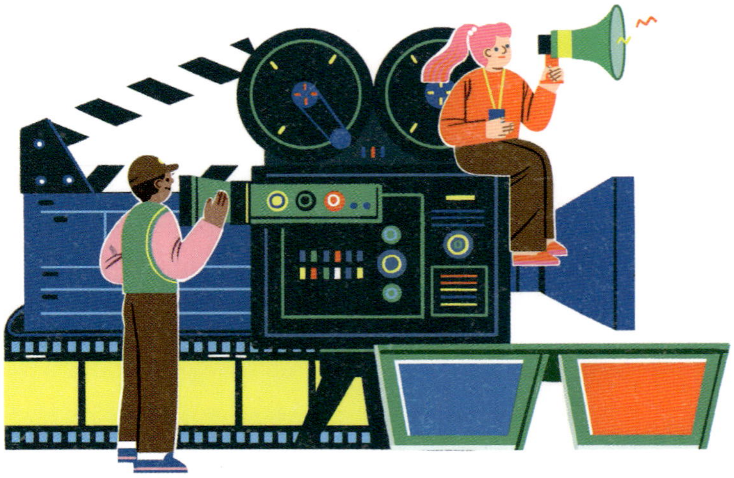